★ SPORTS GREATS ★

TOP 10 TOWERS OF POWER IN BASKETBALL

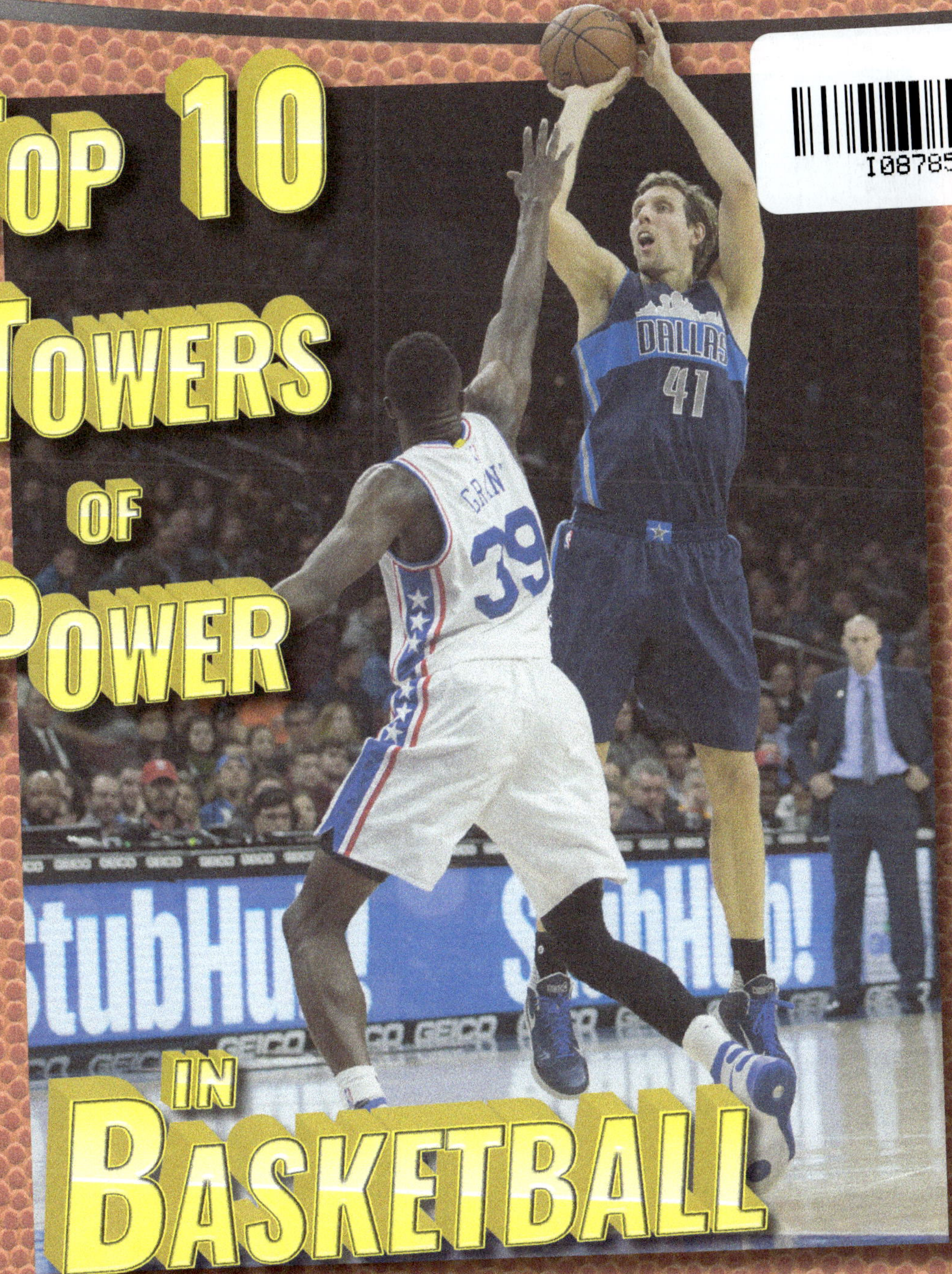

David Aretha

Enslow PUBLISHING

Published in 2017 by Enslow Publishing, LLC.
101 W. 23rd Street, Suite 240, New York, NY 10011

Library of Congress Cataloging-in-Publication Data

Names: Aretha, David, author.
Title: Top 10 towers of power in basketball / David Aretha.
Other titles: Top ten towers of power in basketball
Description: New York : Enslow Publishing, 2017. | Series: Sports greats | Includes bibliographical references and index.
Identifiers: LCCN 2015046100| ISBN 9780766075771 (Library Bound) | ISBN 9780766075733 (Paperback) | ISBN 9780766075757 (6-pack)
Subjects: LCSH: Basketball players—Rating of—United States—Juvenile literature.
Classification: LCC GV884.A1 A69 2017 | DDC 796.3230922—dc23
LC record available at http://lccn.loc.gov/2015046100

Printed in the United States of America

To Our Readers: We have done our best to make sure all website addresses in this book were active and appropriate when we went to press. However, the author and the publisher have no control over and assume no liability for the material available on those websites or on any websites they may link to. Any comments or suggestions can be sent by e-mail to customerservice@enslow.com.

Photos Credits: Cover, p. 1 Mitchell Leff/Getty Images Sport/Getty Images; throughout book, Andrew Rich/E+/Getty Images (basketball texture background); pp. 5, 20 Manny Millan/Sports Illustrated/Getty Images; pp. 7, 16 Focus on Sport/Getty Images; p. 8 Eric Schweikardt/Sports Illustrated/Getty Images; p. 11 Rolls Press/Popperfoto/Getty Images; p. 12 Heinz Kluetmeier/Sports Illustrated/Getty Images; pp. 15, 19 Peter Read Miller/Sports Illustrated/Getty Images; p. 23 Jonathan Daniel/Getty Images Sport/Getty Images; p. 24 PAUL BUCK/AFP/Getty Images; p. 27 Damian Strohmeyer/Sports Illustrated/Getty Images; pp. 28, 32 Sporting News/Getty Images; p. 31 Bill Frakes /Sports Illustrated/Getty Images; p. 35 Barry Chin/The Boston Globe/Getty Images; p. 36 LANCE MURPHEY/AFP/Getty Images; pp. 39, 40 Chris Covatta/Getty Images Sport/Getty Images; p. 43 John W. McDonough/Sports Illustrated/Getty Images; p. 44 Ronald Martinez/Getty Images Sport/Getty Images.

★ Contents ★

★ Introduction ★

In the 1980s, seven-foot Paul Mokeski battled against other centers in the NBA. Broadcaster George Blaha referred to him as Tall Paul, while some critics called him Slo Mo. And that has been the problem with many towers of basketball. Most extremely tall basketball players are not athletic. They're not fast enough to keep up with opponents. They lack the coordination and quickness of smaller players. With their long arms, they struggle to accurately shoot the basketball.

Such was the case with Elmore Morgenthaler, the NBA's first seven-footer. Lacking speed and skill, he averaged just 1.8 points per game in his NBA career. In contrast, the towers of power featured in this book were extraordinarily athletic. Center Bill Russell, who competed in the high jump in college, soared to the heavens to block shots and grab rebounds. Seven-foot Wilt Chamberlain possessed explosive athleticism. He blasted past opposing centers for rim-rattling dunks. In one NBA season, he averaged more than 50 points per game.

Kareem Abdul-Jabbar, seven-foot-two, employed his sky hook to become the NBA's career scoring leader. Shaquille O'Neal, a seven-foot-one 320-pounder, destroyed backboards with his monster slams. Others have used athletic, skillful moves to score inside. For example, Hakeem Olajuwon shed defenders with his dream shake, and Tim Duncan likes to bank shots off the glass. Kevin Garnett, six-foot-eleven, runs the floor and passes like a guard. Dirk Nowitzki, seven feet tall, burns opponents with his long-range shooting.

Before paying tribute to the ten greatest big men of all time, let's look at some other incredible towers:

- George Mikan: The first star center, Mikan dominated the skies beginning in the late 1940s. A giant for his time at six-foot-ten, Mikan caused the creation of the goaltending rule because he rose above the rim to block shots.
- Patrick Ewing and David Robinson: These 1980s and '90s seven-footers were athletic, productive leaders who kept their teams in championship contention for years.
- Gheorghe Muresan and Manute Bol: Muresan and Bol were the tallest players in NBA history. Each was seven-foot-seven.
- Mark Eaton: Though not an NBA great, the seven-foot-four Utah center holds the NBA all-time record with 3.5 blocked shots per game.
- Elvin Hayes: Hayes ranks ninth in NBA history in points (27,313) and fourth in rebounds (16,279). However, the Big E was not considered a good team player.
- Bob Pettit, Bill Walton, Kevin McHale, and Charles Barkley:

All these players were amazing, but only ten made our list as the greatest big men of all time. Here are the towers of power!

Center Patrick Ewing averaged 22.7 points per game and earned 11 All-Star Game invitations during his 15 years with the New York Knicks.

★ Bill Russell ★

Nickname:	None
Team:	Boston Celtics, 1956–1969
Position:	Center
Height:	6'10"
Year of Note:	1961–1962; averaged 23.6 RPG and career-high 18.9 PPG and won NBA MVP Award and NBA title

In 1961–62, center Wilt Chamberlain averaged a record 50.4 points per game (PPG)—an unbelievable feat. Hand him the MVP Award, right? Uh-uh. That season, Boston center Bill Russell earned NBA MVP honors despite averaging just 18.9 PPG. Why?

"There are two types of superstars," Celtics player Don Nelson told the *Boston Globe*. "One makes himself look good at the expense of the other guys on the floor. But there's another type who makes the players around him look better than they are, and that's the type Russell was."

Russell dominated games but not with his scoring. The left-hander struggled with his outside shot and made just 56 percent of his free throws during his NBA career. Instead, Russell excelled through rebounding and defense. The six-foot-ten center averaged 22.5 rebounds per game (RPG) in his thirteen years in the league, which is a figure topped only by Chamberlain. In addition, Bill was the most productive shot blocker in basketball history. Led by Russell and guard Bob Cousy, Boston won eleven NBA championships from 1957 to '69.

As a boy in Oakland, California, Bill couldn't have imagined such success. At age fifteen, he stood six-foot-two and was beanpole thin at 130 pounds. The awkward lad never scored more than 14 points in a high school game. Only one college team offered him a scholarship: the University of San Francisco. He took it. Blossoming with USF, Russell led the Dons to fifty-five consecutive victories and the 1955 and '56 NCAA championships.

Russell (6) and the Celtics went 85–57 in games against Wilt Chamberlain (13). After Wilt was offered a $100,000 salary, the Celtics offered Russell $100,001.

In the NBA, Russell won the MVP Award in 1958, '61, '62, '63, and '65. His rebounding totals were astounding. He once grabbed 51 boards in a game, and he holds NBA records for rebounds in a half (32) and a quarter (19). He shined even brighter in the playoffs

Russell stuffs the Lakers' Bill Hewitt during the 1969 NBA Finals. The Celtics center often blocked ten shots or more in a game.

and averaged 24.9 RPG in his career. Russell used his springy legs and sharp mind to grab those boards. He could sense where each missed shot would carom to, and he put himself in position to grab it.

Russell, who excelled as a high jumper on his college track team, leaped sky high to block shots. He didn't just defend the player he was guarding. He often left his man and went after the player who was driving to the basket. Opponents became hesitant to shoot in fear that Russell would swat the ball back into their face. "The idea is not to block every shot," Russell said. "The idea is to make your opponent *believe* that you might block every shot."

Though blocked shots were not a statistic in Russell's day, he typically averaged 8 to 10 blocks per game, according to NBA referee Earl Strom. How amazing is that? Consider this: Mark Eaton holds the official career record for blocks per game with just 3.5.

In big games, Russell seemingly always came out on top. He played in ten Game 7s in his playoff career and prevailed in every one. In his final three seasons as a player, he served as Boston's head coach, too—winning NBA titles in 1967 and '69.

Due to bad knees, Russell retired in the summer of 1969, and not surprisingly the Celtics' dynasty came to an end. The next season, Boston went 34–48 and finished 26 games out of first place.

★ Wilt Chamberlain ★

Nickname:	*Wilt the Stilt*
Teams:	*Philadelphia Warriors 1959–1962; San Francisco Warriors 1962–1965; Philadelphia 76ers, 1965–1968; Los Angeles Lakers, 1968–1973*
Position:	*Center*
Height:	*7'1"*
Year of Note:	*1961–1962; averaged an NBA record 50.4 PPG while grabbing 25.7 RPG*

Poor Darrall Imhof. With New York Knicks starting center Phil Jordan sick with the flu, Imhof had to guard Philadelphia Warriors center Wilt Chamberlain on March 2, 1962. The six-foot-ten rookie could not contain the seven-foot-one destroyer. Imhof recalled, "After I got my third foul, I said to one of the officials, Willy Smith, 'Why don't you just give him 100 points and we'll all go home?'"

Wilt the Stilt scored so many points that by the third quarter the *New York* fans were chanting, "Give Wilt the ball!" Chamberlain did indeed score 100 points that night, setting an NBA record that has never been approached. He finished the year with a stunning 50.4 points per game (PPG).

Chamberlain wasn't the first seven-footer to play in the NBA. However, he was the first seven-footer with explosive athleticism to wreak havoc on the league. After nearly dying of pneumonia as a child, Wilt developed into a phenomenal athlete. In high school in Philadelphia, he starred in track and field events, such as the long jump, high jump, and shot put. In basketball, his 2,262 career points set a state record and included consecutive games of 74, 78, and 90 points.

Back then, college freshmen weren't eligible to play varsity sports. While a freshman at the University of Kansas, Wilt did get to face the Kansas varsity squad—one of the best teams in the nation—in a scrimmage. "We whipped 'em 81–71," Wilt recalled. "I had 40 or 42 points, about 30 rebounds, about 15 blocks."

After college, Chamberlain played a year with the famous Harlem Globetrotters before signing with the Philadelphia Warriors. In six seasons with the Warriors, he averaged 41.5 points and 25.1 rebounds per game.

Even in the NBA, he still seemed like a grown-up playing against children. In his first six seasons, beginning in 1959–60, he led the league in scoring with averages of 37.6, 38.4, 50.4, 44.8, 36.9,

Wilt leaps to the rafters to block the game's most unblockable shot—a sky hook by seven-foot-two Milwaukee Bucks center Kareem Abdul-Jabbar.

and 34.7 PPG. He paced the league in rebounding in his first four years with the outrageous totals of 27.0, 27.2, 25.7, and 24.3 RPG. All the while, he never seemed to get tired. In 1961–62, he averaged 48.2 minutes per contest even though each game—except those that went into overtime—was only 48 minutes long.

Statisticians didn't keep track of blocked shots back then, but Chamberlain amassed a ton of them. One fan told the *Philadelphia News* what Wilt did to Knicks center Walt Bellamy in 1968: "Bellamy reared back and was slamming the ball down when Wilt put his hand above the top of the rim and knocked the ball off the court. He almost knocked Bellamy off the court, too."

A four-time NBA MVP, Chamberlain led the 1966–67 Philadelphia 76ers and 1971–72 Los Angeles Lakers to NBA championships. He still holds NBA career records for rebounds (23,924) and rebounds per game (22.9), and his 30.07 PPG rank is second to Michael Jordan's 30.12.

After basketball, Wilt played professional volleyball, ran marathons, and competed in tennis and polo. He even hoped to challenge Muhammad Ali in a world heavyweight boxing match. Thankfully for Wilt—or perhaps Ali—that never came to pass.

★ Kareem Abdul-Jabbar ★

Nickname:	None
Teams:	Milwaukee Bucks, 1969–1975 Los Angeles Lakers, 1975–1989
Position:	Center
Height:	7'2"
Year of Note:	1971–1972; led the NBA in scoring at 34.8 PPG while averaging 16.6 RPG

In the Los Angeles Lakers' first game of 1979–80, Kareem Abdul-Jabbar sank a buzzer-beating shot to defeat San Diego. Lakers rookie Magic Johnson—so excited to win his first game—ran up to Kareem and hugged him. In a *Los Angeles Times* interview, teammate Michael Cooper recalled Kareem's response to Magic: "Hey, what are you doing? We've still got eighty-one more games to play!"

That was typical Kareem—always serious business. By his solemn facial expression and slow pace, it looked like he didn't care about winning—or wasn't trying very hard. In the comedy film *Airplane!*, a kid tells him, "I think you're the greatest, but my dad says you don't work hard enough on defense." Abdul-Jabbar responds, "I'm out there bustin' my buns every night!"

For Kareem, the slow but steady pace worked. Over time, he became the most productive basketball player ever. He played the most minutes in NBA history (57,446) and scored the most points (38,387). He ranks third in career rebounds (17,440) and won six NBA MVP Awards. He led the Milwaukee Bucks to the 1971 NBA championship and the Lakers to five NBA titles during the 1980s. And that's just his professional success.

Kareem and point guard Magic Johnson led the Lakers to five NBA titles during the 1980s. Their exciting fast-break style, known as showtime, captured fans' imaginations.

Born as Lew Alcindor in New York City, he grew to six-foot-eight by age thirteen. At Power Memorial Academy, he dominated as the Tower from Power. Alcindor set a New York City record with 2,067 career points, and he led Power Memorial on a seventy-one-game winning streak.

At UCLA, the seven-foot-two center earned National Player of the Year honors in all three of his seasons. He carried the Bruins to three national championships and an overall record of 88–2. Not

Kareem unleashes one of his famous sky hooks. He released it at such a high point that it was almost impossible for opponents to get a finger on the ball.

surprisingly, Milwaukee drafted him with the first overall pick in the 1969 NBA Draft.

A thoughtful, spiritual man, Alcindor converted to Islam and changed his name in 1971. On the court, he averaged 30.4 points in his six years with the Bucks. His sky hook was perhaps "the most awesome weapon in the history of any sport," according to coach Pat Riley.

In *Basketball Legends of All Time,* author Nick Russo described the shot. "To set up the sky hook, Kareem would angle for position along the right side of the key, with his back to the basket. Once set, he could receive a bounce pass, or a high lob pass, and turn over his left shoulder for the shot. The sky hook was delivered in a continuous, almost mechanical, motion, with a final flick of the wrist sending the ball toward the basket. Catch, shoot, swish. Catch, shoot, swish. Automatic."

Abdul-Jabbar released the sky hook from such a high point that no one could block it. When asked how he defended Kareem, six-foot-nine center Johnny Kerr joked, "I'd get real close to him and breathe on his goggles." Another person asked Magic Johnson what he learned by playing with Kareem during his rookie season. Magic's response, "Give him the ball."

Kareem swished the sky hook until 1989, when he finally retired at age forty-one. But before he left that year, he played in his nineteenth All-Star Game—yet another NBA record.

★ Moses Malone ★

Nickname:	Chairman of the Boards
Teams:	Utah Stars (ABA), 1974–1975; Spirits of St. Louis (ABA), 1975–1976; Buffalo Braves, 1976; Houston Rockets, 1976–1982; Philadelphia 76ers, 1982–1986, 1993–1994; Washington Bullets, 1986–88; Atlanta Hawks, 1988–1991; Milwaukee Bucks, 1991–1993; San Antonio Spurs, 1994–1995
Position:	Center
Height:	6'10"
Year of Note:	1982–1983; won the NBA MVP Award and NBA Finals MVP Award

While watching the NBA on television, you couldn't help but notice it—Moses Malone perspired more than anyone else. As he stood at the free throw line and the camera closed in on his face, you could see the sweat pour off his glistening flesh. It was all the result of extreme effort—battling for rebounds, working to establish position, and hounding opponents on defense.

"I may not be the greatest player," Malone said. "But I've always tried to be the hardest worker."

In his twenty-one-year career in the ABA and NBA, Moses amassed 29,580 points (the seventh most in ABA/NBA history) and 17,834 rebounds (third). He was known as Chairman of the Boards. For eight seasons in a row, he led his league in offensive rebounds. Three times he won the NBA MVP Award.

Considering his background, Malone's rise to greatness seems almost miraculous. His father, who was five-foot-six, left the family when Moses was a toddler. His mother, five-foot-two, labored in a meat-packing plant. Somehow, Moses sprouted to six-foot-ten. Through endless hours of playground basketball—sometimes until 2 a.m.—Malone developed into a devastating force. As a senior at Petersburg High School in Virginia in 1973–74, he averaged 36 points, 26 rebounds, and 12 blocked shots per game.

Coaches from more than two hundred colleges tried to recruit him to their schools. Some came to his house uninvited, and one

Malone holds the Larry O'Brien NBA Championship Trophy after leading Philadelphia to the 1983 NBA title. He averaged 25.8 points and 18.0 rebounds in the Finals.

Moses swats a shot by the Lakers' Kurt Rambis. In 1982–83, Malone made the NBA All-Defensive First Team.

was bit by the family's guard dog. One college assistant coach lived at a Petersburg motel for two months while trying to recruit Malone. Moses decided to attend the University of Maryland, but at the last minute he signed a contract with the Utah Stars of the ABA.

As a teenage rookie, Malone averaged 17.5 PPG and 13.6 RPG and earned selection to the ABA All-Star Game. He moved on to the NBA in 1976 and made the All-Star team twelve consecutive years, topping 20 PPG and 11 RPG every season. Six times he led in rebounding with a high of 17.6. In 1981–82 for Houston, he averaged 31.1 PPG and won his second NBA MVP Award.

With Philadelphia a year later, Malone was chosen as league MVP again. Though a quiet man, Moses made a three-word proclamation in 1983 that 76ers fans would never forget. "Fo, fo, fo," he said. He meant that Philadelphia would sweep all three of their playoff series in four games. They then won twelve and lost just one en route to the title. It was Malone's first and only NBA championship.

In 2015, Moses Malone died at age sixty. At his funeral, 76ers legend Charles Barkley recalled how Moses had helped him become a better player and person. Moses Malone Jr. said: "He taught me and my brother so much about life, how to love your family, how to react to anybody that came toward you. He never thought he was any better than anybody. He was friends with the trash man, the janitor, all the way to the star."

Being a good person takes hard work, and no one worked harder than Moses Malone.

★ Hakeem Olajuwon ★

Nickname:	*The Dream*
Teams:	*Houston Rockets, 1984–2001* *Toronto Raptors, 2001–2002*
Position:	*Center*
Height:	*7'0"*
Year of Note:	*1993–1994; became the first player to win the NBA MVP Award, NBA Defensive Player of the Year Award, and NBA Finals MVP Award in same season*

David Robinson knew about the dream shake, but he had no way to stop it. In the 1995 Western Conference Finals, Hakeem Olajuwon went one-on-one against San Antonio's superstar center. Hakeem dribbled to his right, then dribbled the other way with his left hand. He rose for a layup against Robinson then stopped and spun almost all the way around. He faked a second shot. With Robinson rising skyward like a balloon, Hakeem sneaked close to the basket for an easy layup.

The dream shake is "a legendary shot," said Rockets coach Rudy Tomjanovich. "A Hall of Fame shot."

Olajuwon is not only a member of the Basketball Hall of Fame, he ranks among the top handful of centers in NBA history. An athletic seven-footer, Hakeem excelled in all phases of the game. Through 2015, the twelve-time All-Star ranked tenth in career points (26,946), thirteenth in rebounds (13,748), and first in blocked shots (3,830). On the all-time steals lists, he ranked eighth with 2,162. He was the only center among the top fifty.

Olajuwon developed his quick hands and great footwork as a child in Lagos, Nigeria. His favorite sports were handball and soccer. He didn't play basketball until age fifteen, but his parents taught him lessons that would serve him well on the court. "They taught us to be honest, work hard, respect our elders, believe in ourselves," he said. At the University of Houston, Olajuwon led the Cougars to the NCAA Final Four for three straight years. In the 1984 NBA Draft, the Houston Rockets selected him first overall—ahead of Michael Jordan.

Around the basket, Olajuwon employed numerous moves to score on opponents. Here, he takes the Chicago Bulls' Luc Longley to school.

Though the Rockets had been the worst team in the Western Conference in 1983–84, they finished 48–34 in Olajuwon's rookie season. Hakeem averaged 20.6 points and 11.9 rebounds in 1984–85,

Skilled in all aspects of the game, Hakeem recorded 3,058 assists in his career. He also wore cool shoes with his number, 34, written big on the sides.

his first of twelve straight years of at least 20 PPG and 10 RPG. Twice in his career he recorded a quadruple-double: at least 10 points, 10 rebounds, 10 assists, and 10 blocks in a game. Only three other players in NBA history have achieved a quadruple-double—once each.

While immensely talented, Olajuwon worked tirelessly to improve his game. He practiced, refined, and mastered his low-post moves. "My type of basketball is about how to create space, how to maneuver, how to get your shot off," he explained. In addition to the dream shake, he also slayed opponents with the jump hook. From outside, he swished feather-soft jump shots.

Olajuwon reached the pinnacle of his career in the mid-1990s. In 1993–94, he won the NBA MVP Award and led Houston to the NBA title. A year later, he averaged a career-high 27.8 PPG and repeated as league champion. In those two postseasons, he matched up against three of the greatest centers in history: Robinson, Patrick Ewing, and Shaquille O'Neal. In every one of those seventeen games, those Hall of Famers failed to outscore Hakeem.

Even in retirement, Olajuwon made an impact on the court. In the summer of 2011, he taught LeBron James his low-post skills. LeBron improved dramatically because of Hakeem and won the NBA MVP Award and NBA championship the following season.

★ Karl Malone ★

Nickname:	*The Mailman*
Teams:	*Utah Jazz, 1985–2003* *Los Angeles Lakers, 2003–2004*
Position:	*Power forward*
Height:	*6'9"*
Year of Note:	*1996–1997; won NBA MVP Award and led Utah to NBA Finals*

Kareem Abdul-Jabbar is the only NBA player with more points than Karl Malone. But on one play in the 1988 playoffs, Karl creamed Abdul-Jabbar.

Roaring down the court on a fast break, Malone took a pass from Utah point guard John Stockton. With speed, power, and determination, Malone rose up against the seven-foot-two Lakers center. Instead of leaping to contest the shot, Kareem curled up to protect his body and hope he wouldn't be killed. Malone slammed into and jammed over the towering legend. "He goes through you or over you," exclaimed TV analyst Hubie Brown, "and he did *both* of those things to Kareem Abdul-Jabbar."

They called Karl Malone The Mailman because he delivered. Six-foot-nine, athletic, and powerful, he delivered points, rebounds, and victories on a regular basis. He poured in 36,928

Malone slams through two of his 36,928 points, which is the second most in NBA history. His 25.0 points per game rank thirteenth of all time.

Malone's exercise routine included two hours on a Stairmaster, an hour of sprint drills, and running up stadium steps. And that doesn't include his time in the weight room.

points—just 1,429 short of Kareem's total. He grabbed 14,968 rebounds (sixth of all-time), and he powered Utah to the playoffs in all of his eighteen seasons there. As for slam dunks, they numbered in the thousands. "What excites me the most," Malone said half-jokingly, "is when a coach calls a timeout and chews out his forward because I just dunked on his head."

Malone built his muscles on a farm in hot and humid Summerfield, Louisiana. With eight siblings and no father around, Karl had to man up at an early age. He fished, hunted, baled hay, and chopped trees. He and his brother Terry also did fun things they shouldn't have, such as riding pigs as if they were horses. Karl's grades were so low as a freshman at Louisiana Tech that he was ineligible to play that season. He then earned all-conference honors three straight years. In the 1985 NBA Draft, the Utah Jazz selected him thirteenth overall.

For eighteen seasons, John Stockton and Malone became the most productive teammates in NBA history. The point guard became the first NBA player with 10,000 assists—then pushed that number to 15,806—with thousands going to Malone. Not only did Stockton pass to his locomotive forward on the fast break, he frequently fed him close to the basket. Malone was so strong that he could back his defender closer and closer to the rim then score on him with a variety of moves. Often, the only way opponents could stop Malone was to foul him, but The Mailman delivered at the foul line, as well. His 9,787 converted free throws are an NBA record.

For seventeen consecutive seasons, he averaged more than 20 PPG—often while playing hurt. Jazz strength coach Mark McKown called Karl's commitment to fitness extremely obsessive. He was named First Team All-NBA eleven times, and he won the NBA MVP Award in 1997 and 1999. Also outspoken about everything from basketball to politics, Malone frequently made the NBA All-Interview Team.

The only thing The Mailman didn't deliver was an NBA championship. He and Stockton led the Jazz to the NBA Finals in 1997 and '98, but they lost both years to Michael Jordan and the Chicago Bulls.

After retirement, Malone returned to his roots and moved back to Louisiana with his wife and kids. He ran a timber company and once again chopped down trees.

★ Shaquille O'Neal ★

Nickname:	Shaq
Teams:	Orlando Magic, 1992–1996; Los Angeles Lakers, 1996–2004; Miami Heat, 2004–2008; Phoenix Suns, 2008–2009; Cleveland Cavaliers, 2009–2010; Boston Celtics, 2010–2011
Position:	Center
Height:	7'1"
Year of Note:	1999–2000; won NBA MVP Award and NBA Finals MVP Award

Shaquille O'Neal couldn't stop the destruction. During a massive dunk while playing for Louisiana State, he snapped the rim almost completely off. In practice one day, with his opponent yelling, "Let me see your best," he ripped off the rim and shattered the backboard. With his Shaq attacks in the NBA, he twice pulled down the whole backboard. Because of O'Neal, the NBA had to make the structures stronger—or Shaq-proof.

Shaquille O'Neal stood over seven feet tall and weighed 320 pounds. He was so big and strong that he simply backed up like a truck and dunked on opposing centers. In his career, he scored 28,596 points (sixth all-time) and won four NBA championships. Late in games, some teams resorted to Hack-a-Shaq. In other words, since they couldn't stop him, they fouled him to send him to the free throw line. There, he typically made only one of two

O'Neal throws down a monster jam for the Orlando Magic. In 2015, Shaq's 15-year-old son, Shareef O'Neal, was already dunking like dad.

shots. "Me shooting 40 percent at the foul line is just God's way of saying that nobody's perfect," he said.

The stepson of an Army sergeant, O'Neal began his dominance at Robert G. Cole High School in San Antonio, Texas. He jammed on kids half his size, rebounded every ball in sight, and won 68 of 69 games. After his two years at Louisiana State—where he earned National Player of the Year honors—the Orlando Magic drafted him first overall in the 1992 NBA Draft.

Kobe Bryant (left) and O'Neal didn't always get along, but together they led the Lakers to three straight NBA titles. Note the Superman tattoo on Shaq's bicep.

Even in the NBA, Shaq was too big to contain. Besides dunking several times a game, he beat defenders with short hook shots or simple layups. His shots were so close to the basket that he led the league in field goal percentage ten times. In his first thirteen seasons, he averaged at least 21 PPG and 10 RPG every year.

The fifteen-time All-Star paced the NBA in scoring in 1994–95 with the Magic (29.3 PPG) and 1999–2000 with the Lakers (29.7). From 2000 to 2002, Shaq and Kobe Bryant led Los Angeles to three straight NBA championships. In 2005–06, he teamed with LeBron James to win an NBA title with Miami.

Along the way, Shaq entertained teammates and fans with his jokes and provocative comments. He referred to himself as The Big Aristotle. In his book *Shaq Talks Back*, he wrote: "I stole a quote from that Greek philosopher cat: 'Excellence is not a singular act, but a habit. You are what you repeatedly do.'"

During and after his career, O'Neal remained in the public eye. He recorded several rap albums; appeared in numerous commercials, films, and television shows; and even produced a TV movie called *The Love Shaq*. O'Neal not only graduated from college, he went on to earn a master of business degree and then a doctorate degree in education. Many consider him a terrific role model for kids.

"I'm a weird big guy," he said. "Doing rapping, doing movies. Do a lot of stuff." But, he added, "[I] always do things the right way."

★ Kevin Garnett ★

Nickname: *The Big Ticket*
Teams: *Minnesota Timberwolves, 1995–2007, 2015–2016; Boston Celtics, 2007–2013; Brooklyn Nets, 2013–2015*
Position: *Power forward*
Height: *6'11"*
Year of Note: *2007–2008: named NBA Defensive Player of the Year and helped lead Boston to the NBA championship*

Could a player go directly from high school to the NBA? That's what fans wondered when Kevin Garnett made that transition in 1995. That season, he became the first high school player in twenty years to go pro.

As a rookie with Minnesota, the six-foot-eleven teenager proved he belonged. In one game that season, he soared above the rim and blocked a shot by Houston's Eldridge Recasner. The rejected ball bounced to the Rockets' Sam Mack, who then missed a jump shot. Garnett snatched the rebound. He dribbled once and fired a pass to Terry Porter to start the fast break. Porter dribbled up court and spotted Kevin flying down the left side. He passed it to the big man, who soared to the heavens and slammed it home. The fans went crazy. In a span of twelve seconds, Garnett had illustrated why Minnesota had drafted him fifth overall—he could do everything on the basketball court.

By 2015, Garnett had played in fifteen All-Star Games—the most in history by a forward. He had won the NBA MVP Award, NBA Defensive Player of the Year Award, and NBA championship. All the while, coaches praised him for his work ethic, passion to win, and unselfish play. "He's great for our game," said NBA coach Larry Brown. "He's as good a teammate as you could possibly have and as great a kid to coach as you could ever want."

Garnett has always taken comfort in basketball. Growing up poor in South Carolina, Kevin didn't have his father in his life. He

A tremendous individual talent, Garnett achieved greatness because he worked well with teammates. Here he gives guard Rajon Rondo a friendly head pat.

Garnett is so intense that he often howls on the court—just like timber wolves do in the forests of Minnesota.

lived with his mother and two sisters. "When I didn't have a friend, when I was lonely, I always knew I could grab that orange pill and go hoop," Kevin said. "If things weren't going right, I could make a basket and feel better."

For his senior year, Garnett transferred to Farragut Career Academy in Chicago. Never before had fans seen a near-seven-footer play like Kevin. He could soar two feet above the rim, run the floor like a small forward, pass like a guard, and swish turnaround jumpers.

With the Timberwolves, KG made the NBA All-Star Game in just his second season. In his twelve years in Minnesota, he averaged more than 20 PPG nine times and led the league in rebounding four straight seasons. During his 2003–04 MVP season, he set career highs with 24.2 points and 13.9 rebounds per game.

Garnett, who played with tremendous energy and passion, carried the T'Wolves to the playoffs for eight straight years. He earned a reputation as a winner, which is why Boston acquired him in 2007. In his first year with the Celtics, he helped power them to the NBA title. Celtics teammate Sam Cassell said that Kevin "cares about your feelings. He respects the last guy on the team." And, he added, "He's the best competitor I've ever been around."

In 2015, Garnett returned to the T'Wolves—the team he had joined twenty years earlier. In his first game back, on February 25, fans welcomed him with a thunderous standing ovation. "When you think of the Timberwolves, you think of Kevin Garnett," said teammate Andrew Wiggins. "That's the first thing that comes up."

★ Tim Duncan ★

Nickname:	*Slam*
Team:	*San Antonio Spurs, 1997–present*
Position:	*Power forward/center*
Height:	*6'11"*
Year of Note:	*2002–2003; averaged 23.3 PPG and 12.9 RPG, won NBA MVP Award and NBA Finals MVP Award*

He moves like lightning and slams with thunder. But it took the force of a hurricane to actually get him onto a basketball court.

In his legendary career with San Antonio, Tim Duncan has made the All-NBA and All-Defensive teams fifteen times each. He has led the Spurs to the playoffs nineteen years in a row as of 2015 and won five NBA championships. He can shoot, score, pass, rebound, defend, lead, and win as well as any big man in the game. "No question he's the greatest power forward ever," said former teammate David Robinson. "It's hard to compare anyone to Tim. He's in a class by himself."

Yet if it weren't for Hurricane Hugo, Duncan might never have played basketball.

Growing up in St. Croix, US Virgin Islands, Tim was an elite-level swimmer. By age thirteen, he ranked among the world's best in his age group and dreamed of competing in the Olympics—a

Duncan scores near the basket with a variety of crafty moves.

Tim is the only player ever named to the All-NBA and All-Defensive Teams in every one of his first thirteen seasons.

real possibility. But then came hurricane Hugo, which roared through St. Croix and destroyed the only Olympic-sized swimming pool in Tim's area. His coach moved swim practice to the ocean, but since Tim was afraid of sharks, he stopped going. With the death of his mother, Ione, he quit competitive swimming altogether.

Tall, strong, and athletic, Tim decided to give basketball a try. Soon he became a dominant force on the court, and Wake Forest University offered him a scholarship. There, he would fulfill his mother's dying wish for him: stay in school four years and earn a college degree. Along the way, the soft-spoken Demon Deacon became the first NCAA player ever with 1,500 points, 1,000 rebounds, 400 blocked shots, and 200 assists. "If you're looking for a fearless warrior who plays his A game every single night, you'd have a hard time finding anybody better than Timmy in any era," said Wake Forest head coach Dave Odom.

Chosen number one overall in the 1997 NBA Draft, Duncan teamed with superstar center David Robinson. Together, they won NBA championships in 1999 and 2003. In the title-clinching game in 2003, Duncan tallied 21 points, 20 rebounds, 10 assists, and eight blocked shots. Without Robinson, Duncan led the Spurs to NBA titles in 2005, 2007, and 2014.

Quiet but deadly—like a shark—Duncan has numerous moves around the basket. Highly intelligent, he puts himself into proper position for rebounds and defense. He has a soft touch on his shot, and he passes like a guard.

"He has every move," NBA star Carlos Boozer told *USA Today*. "He has poise. He never gets rattled. You can send a double-team at him, but he'll pass out of it. If he has single coverage, he'll face you up and shoot off the glass, get the layup, spin move baseline, right hook, left hook, fadeaway. He can do whatever he wants down there."

Through his first ten seasons, Duncan averaged 21.8 PPG. By 2015, he ranked eighth in career rebounds and sixth in blocked shots. He even achieved his Olympic dream—although not in the water. In 2004, he represented USA Basketball at the Summer Olympics in Athens, Greece.

★ Dirk Nowitzki ★

Nickname:	*The Dunking Deutschman*
Teams:	*Dallas Mavericks, 1998–present*
Positions:	*Power forward/center*
Height:	*7'0"*
Year of Note:	*2010–2011; won NBA championship and NBA Finals MVP Award*

Dirk Nowitzki picked a terrible time to get sick. For thirteen seasons, he had fallen short of the NBA title. And in 2011, his Dallas Mavericks stood at a critical point. They trailed the Miami Heat two games to one in the NBA Finals, and a loss in Game 4 would be almost fatal. But how could Dirk muster the energy to compete on this Tuesday night in Dallas? He suffered from a sinus infection, had hardly slept the night before, and burned with a fever that approached 102 degrees.

Reaching deep within himself, he found a way. After Miami took a 69–65 lead through three quarters, the German-born star scored 10 points in the final period—including an important driving lay-in with fourteen seconds left. Dallas won 86–83 to stay alive even though Dirk felt half dead. "Just battle it out," he said after the game. "This is the Finals. You have to go out there and compete and try your best for your team. So that's what I did." The

Mavericks won the series in six games, and Dirk was named the NBA Finals MVP.

Nowitzki grew up in Wurzburg, West Germany, a city that had been bombed mercilessly during World War II. Dirk had all the physical advantages to star in basketball. His mother had played on West Germany's national basketball team, and his father had been a world-class handball player. Dirk sprouted to seven feet tall, yet he remained a remarkably well-coordinated athlete.

German basketball star Holger Geschwindner became Nowitzki's personal coach. He taught his student that "basketball is a dance," Dirk said. Geschwindner made him learn a musical

While Dallas teammate Jason Kidd (right) hoists the NBA championship trophy in 2011, Nowitzki shows off the NBA Finals MVP Award, which he earned.

The most prolific shooter ever among centers, Dirk is the only big man to make more than 1,500 three-point shots.

instrument and read physics books as part of his basketball training. He also helped Dirk become one of the greatest shooting and passing seven-footers the game had ever seen.

In 1998, the Milwaukee Bucks selected Dirk with the ninth pick in the NBA Draft. The Mavericks immediately traded for Nowitzki, who led them to the playoffs every year from 2000–01 to 2011–12. In each of those twelve seasons, he averaged more than 20 points per game. Coaches raved about his court awareness and slick passing. He excelled as a rebounder and scored easily around the basket. But notably, he slayed opponents with his outside shot.

Releasing his jumper from high in the sky, Dirk was indefensible—sometimes unstoppable. He not only swished short and mid-range shots, he buried as many 151 three-pointers in a season. In several years, he averaged more than 40 percent from three-point land. Those who fouled him paid the price, as he shot nearly 90 percent at the free throw line.

In 2005–06, Nowitzki averaged a career-high 26.6 PPG and scored 50 points against Phoenix in a playoff game. In 2006–07, Dirk and star guards Steve Nash and Michael Finley led Dallas to a 67–15 record. That season, he became the first big man ever to shoot 50 percent from the floor, 40 percent from three-point territory, and 90 percent from the free throw line. He was named the NBA MVP.

Dirk, who entered the 2015–16 season with 28,119 points, was striving to become the sixth NBA player to score 30,000. On November 11, he nailed five of six threes and finished with 31 points. At age thirty-seven, he was still unstoppable.

★ Glossary ★

ABA—American Basketball Association, a professional league that rivaled the NBA from 1967 to 1976.

baseline—The out-of-bounds line behind the basket.

boards—Another word for rebounds.

dynasty—A period of several years in which a team dominates by winning multiple league championships.

fadeaway jumper—A jump shot taken while falling backwards; such a shot is difficult for the defender to block.

Final Four—The four remaining teams in the NCAA men's basketball tournament—and women's.

goaltending—A violation in which a player interferes with a shot when it is on its downward arc toward the basket.

jump hook—A one-handed shot in which the player extends one arm out to the side and over the head toward the basket while jumping.

jump shot—A shot made while jumping and releasing the ball at the peak of the jump.

key—The rectangular area in front of the basket.

low post—A nonspecific area close to the basket; big players like to get the ball in the low post so they can shoot a close-range shot.

post up—To play near the basket with one's back to the rim.

power forward—Typically a larger, stronger forward who plays close to the basket.

scholarship—An amount of money that a school gives to a student for his or her education.

varsity—The top-level team at a high school, college, or university.

★ Further Reading ★

Books

Doeden, Matt. *Wilt Chamberlain.* Minneapolis, MN: Twenty-First Century Books, 2011.

Donnelly, Patrick. *The Best NBA Centers of All Time.* Edina, MN: ABDO Publishing, 2015.

Donnelly, Patrick. *The Best NBA Forwards of All Time.* Edina, MN: ABDO Publishing, 2015.

Grange, Michael. *Basketball's Greatest Stars.* Richmond Hill, Ontario, Canada: Firefly Books, 2013.

Thornley, Stew. *Kevin Garnett: Champion Basketball Star.* Berkeley Heights, NJ: Enslow Publishers, 2013.

Thornley, Stew. *Tim Duncan: Champion Basketball Star.* Berkeley Heights, NJ: Enslow Publishers, 2013.

Websites

Basketball Reference

basketball-reference.com

Includes statistics on every player in NBA history.

Jr. NBA

jr.nba.com

Sections include "Skills and Drills," "About the Game," "Fun Zone," and more.

National Basketball Association

nba.com

Loaded with everything NBA: player profiles, scores, stats, standings, news, and highlight videos, as well as "Kids Club Fun and Games."

★ Index ★